A Pair of Three

Claire Crowther

A Pair of Three

Shearsman Books

First published in the United Kingdom in 2022 by
Shearsman Books Ltd
PO Box 4239
Swindon
SN3 9FN

Shearsman Books Ltd Registered Office
30–31 St. James Place, Mangotsfield, Bristol BS16 9JB
(this address not for correspondence)

www.shearsman.com

ISBN 978-1-84861-821-3

ACKNOWLEDGEMENTS

Thanks to *Blackbox Manifold, Perverse, prototype, Scintilla, Shearsman, Stand, Tentacular, The Fortnightly Review, The Next Review, The North, Under the Radar* for publishing some of the poems in this collection. Thanks to Sidekick Books for including 'A Sweet Accord' in their Hipflask anthology.

I would like to thank the Stockwell poets (Anne Berkeley, Rhona McAdam, Sue Rose, Tamar Yoseloff) and the Helyar poets (Fiona Benson, Patrick Brandon, John Clarke, Julia Copus, Jane Draycott, Carrie Etter, Annie Freud, Jenny Lewis) for their regular help and reminders that writing poetry does not have to be done alone. David Thompson is a meticulous first responder and has saved me from many blunders; Linda Black gives rigorous and sympathetic support whenever I ask; Carrie Etter is a friend of extensive wisdom without whom I could not do.

Most specially, thanks to my stepdaughters and Keith
for bearing with my trespass on their loss.

Thanks beyond thanks to Jude.

Contents

A PAIR OF THREE

JU DE LUNE

EPILOGUERY

EPITAPHERY

for Judith Barnham 1942–1994

The silence of eternity,
Interpreted by love!
        —John Greenleaf Whittier

Put me not to shame,
Because I am
Thy clay that weeps, thy dust that calls.
    —George Herbert

EPIGRAPHERY

A Pair of Three

He goes out later than a new wife wants
up to The Lookout.
Does he meet someone?

He keeps two photos of his weddings –
each pair of us –
her him me.

I wonder about the singularity
of a pair of three –
an us.

It's late. No, partner, not too late. Still
one of us is late: she finds him
in The Lookout.

The Visitor

While he was out I read a book.
I had to rest that day.
Then I heard a key in the lock
and steps in the hallway.

How could there be somebody there?
Yet listen: rustling bags,
clinking cup and running tap,
the snap of the kettle's plug.

Someone in her own place
settled with her tea.
Someone opened an old book
and sat relaxed like me.

I heard humming through the house
and skipping up the stair
yet when I held out my hand
I touched nothing there.

Later we sat down to eat
and talked about the day.
He shared difficult things but I...
I thought but couldn't say.

Foot and Stair

'The dredful fotyng doth so often change'
    —John Lydgate, *Danse Macabre, 1426*

We came as strangers to this wormholed wood,
pile on clay,
the dreadful footings of the danse macabre.

We chose high:
an attic – stone-sunk windows overlook
dunes of roofs

silted from inland seas. We tiptoed up
to our room
on treads so short a slight foot could over-

reach – here imps
peg the windings, and demons of tightness
trick to trip.

I took care not to lose my footing scaling
wooden hills
and at the top landing steadied: below

were fruit-full
arthritic fig trees, down where old stories
would be told.

Over

How could he guess she was fixing
adamant on that view?

How could she lie so quiet
when she had mending to do?

How could he search for a vase
while she made him a widower?

How could visitors ask for tea
weak   strong   sugar?

How could she turn as she lay
and hold to her daughters' gaze?

How could I step in and sit down
wordfilled in her room?

An Apprehension of Gingerbread

A barrage of boxes in the hall.
The mattress had torn on one corner.
It bled lead-grey wool.

Her picture lay dazed in the stairwell,
its unprotected glaze smashed against
a rat's tail cactus.

After he'd carried her to the shed
glass particles gleamed along the way
back through red roses,

the front garden's upright standards fixed
in that grave yard of home. He locked up.
Started his car. Fled.

AFTERYEARN

Oh, Why Did She Leave Him in the Park of Gone?

In the morning he packs his purple tent.
That good grey bole will hold
his bags and books.

He wears jute sacking and his head is bare.
His long hair is matted
like a full mind.

He walks beyond walls, daughters, job and wealth,
beyond safe kerbs that cut
into the cold.

Castle Lane, Hobs Moat

How dry
that moat.
No Fridays with their faith in fish.

Why walk
these trails?
A fracas of winged seeds chokes him.

How come
his door,
his glazed porch can't hear her knocking?

Her kiss
was their
wafer-thin communion. Our keeps

are in
the heart.
So where will his homing spirit go?

Moving and Shaking

Who found him?

Out limping   Gloveless   Hatless

Who gave him summer to eat?

Casseroles frighten December

Why did I need to knit?

A warm moss-stitch sanctuary

Who saw he had a calling?

Sun isn't threatened by cold

Whose breath silvered his lamenting?

Newfoundwife

The Physics of Coincidence

The red carriage

of fuchsia swung its bells to his foot falling
                towards my step.
His arm winged out to a parked car. My curls swung.
                If two atoms

share an electron and bond in one body
                in one compass-
ion of matter swaying with so much co-
                incidence direct-

ionless as the atoms that long for time
                to herd its lengths
into shocks that rope and weave each to each...
                then there's no which.

Mussels at Fisherman's Wharf, San Francisco Bay

in memory of Gerson Goldhaber

If I had asked Gerson what he knew
while we watched the sun's weight flatten Alcatraz –
if I had said: Have you physicists
observed the recognition these creatures feel
for the rocks they cling to ... But I asked:
What's your specialism? What is it you do?

So he outlined his job: to research the end
of the universe. To ask whether
our matter will continue to expand
as unlike a finish as one could hope.
Or will the world shrink? His graphs showed expansion.

While Keith dreams of sun and her, I dream
dark matter can stream memories from tachyons
that glow and flow to and fro in soul physics.

We parted in the dark. Look, iridescence
hasps wave-washed rocks clasped by salt water.
Though I'm freshwater – *unionida* – yet
Keith stayed rapt and homesick by the bay.

He Missed Her Again

He missed her
when something unsure of itself
was laid on the sill to dry.

A mild shade.
A droop of water-green grapes
picked unswollen. As they dried

caramel
sweetmeat – autumn – flared back through
summer to pale spring running

from winter
as colours do. He recalled
that they walked the beech-leaving

lane talking
talking talking deciding
to make a child while the sun

spangled her.
Golden photons reflected
from the drying brown beech leaves.

He saw her.
Should I have spoken? No words
fall this powerful season.

Coming to Terms

He (*The Widower*) watches a red sky.
Bricks of invisible bungalows catch at shine
and far-away elm trees are swathed in it.

Hewidow he is.
Herhusband I call him.

The sky refuses to infuse us tonight.
Though I am warm with blood,
it pulls us to a cold latitude.

I could call him *My Widowman*.
She could say *My Searcherman*.

All we who are titled
are entitled to what's ours.

A Sweet Accord

i *Noticing odd things while sleepy...*

Notably: he's fingering the pink embroidery on the bedspread.
    He thinks his first wife bought this warm cover.

Notably: what he wrote long ago is treasure:
    tiny books
    dated spines

ii *His fictional diary...*

2 Sunday: Varying views on life & death keeping me awake:
    who widowed... who widow-wed... who widowered...

15 Saturday: Ju? Remember this bedspread? Chosen for its
pink embroidered water avens?
    & there's something else...

19 Wednesday: We were never obnoxious with each other!

27 Thursday: Thinking of you

27 Thursday: Must go now

31 Sunday: Oncewife?

31 Sunday: Listen! Dark is different! Dark matter has no sound

31 Sunday: There's only light
    I was sunwed I won't unwed
    You're something!

31 Sunday: Are you even here?
>Can't you watch with me a while?
>Ju?

iii *A widower's new wife must clarify…*

Fortuitously
>some matters are curiously clear in the small hours.

For example
>that I remember while you

Forget
>that this bedspread with its distinctive drooping heads
>>of water avens
>was chosen by me to celebrate
>your proposal – though that was a while back.

Forgotten!
>Proposals are life-changing!
>But when you think of our pair of three don't panic

For
>while I'm here you need never

Forego
>my

Forbearance
>and, life and death apart, I want to be at peace with you…

The Welcome

She stood at our front door –
and more than that
I heard her knock.

My husband's late first wife –
and more than that
his first true love.

Her boots were hard and worn –
softer than that,
her scarf afloat.

I could not calm my mind –
despite that I
unlatched the door.

THIS AND THAT

Those Keys

I am locked out.
He knows he has forgotten something.
Listen to him check, hose,
his secateurs?

Lavender sprays swathe
the long infirm necks and plush-red crowns
of bergamot.
How come odd old

plants have been let
to wane: skinny verbena, mauve sage?
Now I am left,
as we must each be left,

that bad thing I
would not face – I
have to think about it.
I'll kneel to think, I'll pluck back thick stalks

crowding a fennel thread.
The street light streams
its orange like hemerocallis
and wet soil shines.

Two mice eyes glint.
Fox rat death lurk.
He clutches the cold keys while he hums:
'Where has she gone?'

Home

The brownfield behind our estate is thick
    with vervain
        wild garlic
            pulmonaria.

Thieves eat peach buds and clever criminals
    clip privet leaves.
        We three
            are curators

of this enterprise. In kitchen catch-ups
    or in the blue shed
        we plan
            new works.

We can disagree. At times one of us
    retires to the small
        meeting room
            (once known

as the spare bedroom). When s/s/he comes back
    the others say, 'Hi.'
        'How are you?'
            'Are you OK?'

This Shaking Ground

Once in a hotel a tidal
billow shook. I couldn't
stand still for underground
breakers.

Undulating as those stairs were
our room was worse. A berth
in the hold of waves swelled
to fall,

and he, my stay, my banister,
my grab rail, he said: Yes,
I feel the room roll. Up
down up,

the treadling seawater swayed on
under that undocked bed.
Folie à deux, à deux,
à deux.

I Ask These Questions on a Country Walk

I'm no country person
I don't know
why

fern ochres will unfurl arteries

why

sorrel seeds will rash red

why

a beck will froth-crook over rocks

why

ranked crosswort will fiddle with air while either side of the stream
    green weed will strip trails of tree bones

why

grey fence will veil the lane

why

that stone will shroud with moss butterbur and ox-eye daisies

why

this field will spurt wild blood
    will be blood meadow

Lost in Thought

This world is 'nothing but one great Machine' David Hume would retort were he driving today down an M road to a Business of Joy Area. In the car park there is buying polishing and taking photographs of the characteristic lean against the driver's door. But not too near the road. Cars – the world's lesser machines – could be more highly coloured yet softer on impact. Besides she can't beat about the bushes here for ever.

The dead are not doing what they are told. There is looking for them calling and messaging. Sometimes she hides tiny as the ghost spider *Anyphaenidae*. Sometimes, like Dreadnoughtus the dinosaur, she overwhelms loving bodies. *Ten nine eight I'm coming to find you.* 'The idea of a comparison of words or mental representations with objects is a senseless one.' So says philosopher du jour Hilary Putnam.

Is seriousness a growing problem for outdoor bowls? There is studying opponents calling to officials and denigrating bagger totals. St John in Revelation warns that those elders who survive a plague do not repent of their fornications. *Where are you?* Nor indeed of other more communally-based stress-solvers. *Where are you?*

Consider: there is redaction smoothing over or even erasure. *Are you under here?* As Susan B Anthony joked in an era of misogyny if a woman cannot vote due to being represented in law by her husband/father/etc then her husband/etc should hang for the murder she will no doubt be driven to commit. Could someone help us recover her lost soul?

Yet the thoughtful remind us that for the human being mortality is one hundred percent. There is spending being spent and having been spent. *Hold it right now.* And then again Søren Kierkegaard explained thrillingly – explanations engender doubt. Did somebody say don't overthink it? Let's just go for – and while here never let go of – the epiphany. *Hold hands till we get to the gate. Don't ever hide again. Not funny.* Good hiding good hiding beaten heart.

The Us

I ran downstairs
and said 'I've just thought:
We are random.
The you and I.
The she and you.
The she and I.
The us.'

'Here,' Keith said –
      he pushed aside his coffee,
      picked up the stapler he'd been using to hold together
      his notes on this and that background to this
      or that experiment –
'Here is a set of steel links'
      pointing to a line of staples.

I felt I was the wall
the molecules of his ordering thought
bounced against.

'And here' he said 'are the staples coming and going
gripping each other
and going
until...'

'No' I said and ran into the kitchen.
'Too many meanings!
Food is staples.
Look: are eggs random?'

'Oh I'm going to work on a paper,' he said,

and passing me as I stood by the fridge:
'Random interactions of molecules
led to increasingly complex molecules.
They became more and more complex
until they could start to replicate.'

And he hardly stopped at the door to say:
'Order in the universe increased tremendously
until love became an evolutionary principle.'

I ran upstairs.

A PAIR OF THREE

We Shine Love So Hard

that we exchange our selves
in our day's reflections.
We wear each other's jacket
of worry. We walk thoughtfully

when there's a sudden onset
of mist. We place our soles
away from the skew of camber.
Careful. I can't see what will

betray your step. Or what will slip
under mine. Sometimes
the fog seems so much like
a mortal illness

that I hear: *Non lasciarmi –*
don't leave me – and hear
you murmur: *Ecco eccomi.*

Let Those Who are Entitled Say *I*

Waswife

Wifeinhere

Pastwife not passed over

Nightwife

Bidewife

Pastwife not passed over

Stillwife

Everwife

Pastwife not passed over

*And let her who heard say **I***
*   **I** heard her*

I Think Heaven Must Co-opt Hell for Help

Evening. A cathedral tucked down a close
of three-bed Gothics.
Candled, vaulted. Three dunnocks chat by the kerb.
At the iron gate
gargoyles guard a saint who throws wide her warm arms.
She holds her symbol:
her tray of lost breast. Her chestnut ringlets shine
shaved off and regrown.
The worst enjambment of my life is this turn
through a dead woman's door.

The Poet Longs for Hyperbole
on the Anniversary of Jude's Loss

branch bole and leaves
aren't stuffed with sun
purple pigeons on our fence have shrunk

I should expand my words at least overdo 'let's have less *or*' and
'up the *and*'

so: extraness is bursting through big cloud
dearth
is now dismissed on earth

out thin binaries

nor shall I say 'just dust'
nor shall I whisper
the concrete 'never'

Restricted View, Dresden

Symphony of Joy, Beethoven

Fifty feet below me in Our Lady's basilica,
the conductor walks in unseen
by us up here

and players stand in respect for arms that remember sleights
of composition. Her patterns
and their outcomes,

exactly as she predicts, are so close that you can't hear
space between baton and prelude.
Now, one by one,

we stand up to see the concert, to hear our histories.
We can't go on imagining
how she drives joy.

We stand glad to hold each our own church-worth of replaced notes
like postwar rubble women sifting
shelled stones of love.

Restless

I've been measuring the strength of a storm's hands.
The virus has raged in my husband's lungs.
Anything is breakable by blows.
I've been urging
snowdrops to press closer to the earth
while whatever's breathless longs for them.

Whirling wind, you ruffling rushing gale, sweep out.
You're nothing but our inhalations.
Breath batters us to blast more through us.
We share
air and sigh so much. I hear his breath
go and come and calm. Let's sleep till dawn.

Helicity from the Library Basement

The stair began where I sat
       and circled to the top. Then nipped the flank
of blue sky through a lantern.

It began at my chair when
       I turned the three hundredth or so page. That
was the second I saw. Soared

up two floors. Swooshing steps flashed
       into someone else's trajectory
of unknowingness. Just bulk

of back bearing a book bag
       as usual. One by one they climbed past
the other rockface readers.

I saw sun through the risers.
       Big universe whose self I took. Small bang
in my head was hers. I gave

as would a white-footed mouse
       share ticks with any human: ticks and selves
testimonies to hostage

or vectors swirling disease.
       I'm back by the stacks. Still the long straight shelves
stand. Arc over arc of oak

banisters run floor to roof.
       Books, stop staring. I've told you. And you, words,
whirl. You're a choir. You'll be heard.

Mourning Her

Her pointing
at the blue pattern looping through orange wool:

'You're the one
to explain this. Your metaphors.' Me speechless.

My husband
in bed waking. His recognition of her. His welcoming.

His steepling
hands like prayer guides. He gasping seeing a goddess crouching

at the end
of the week of me buying a rug. (Our bed being high. Me falling.

Rugs saving
pain.) She seeing me rising from the pillows as he is seeing her.

Me kneeling
wiping up water spilling on tufts bending under rushing knees
            and feet.

Us being
sustainable. Me thinking:

Are we being electrons, the one electron
shooting back and forth in time? Or walking in one being?

There being
others in us making our whole?

My feet freezing. She on her haunches
looking at

what she is looking from. Her big eyes. My tough chin.
His praising. Me settling

back in bed. A streak of blue pushing through our blurry
glazing. Morning.

I Saw a Crowd of Weird Birds

fall to the ground. Ground
down by ghosts they turned away. Away
the birds went. I turned back. None. No one
can convince me that you're not. Not
while those birds might bring their flock back.

Find out confined out
in as much *always* as there is there
if there is no there there
or no no end.

Then make your comeback. Come back here.

Butterfly on the Clary Sage

She stared from the frizzled leaves
and pale mauve bracts,

and we said, 'Look. Look at her.'
Peacock pausing

beside us. How she hovered
in our 'Stop stop'

of sudden comprehension.
Not once showing

four frightened eyes as peacocks
might. Is meaning

what she makes when she means
to show herself?

Keith Explains his Single Existence Proof While I Sing

Werwidow Werwidow
What is your Werlife

Beyond doubt
Beyond death
There's nothing

If you choose a Werwidow
You'll have some Werstrife

But find just one
Example of existence –
Life after death becomes a fact

For there's no Werlover
Lets go his Werwife

JU DE LUNE

Ju de Lune

I think she's dancing through our streets alone
or hauntering
on wet elm leaves.

Under pylons, past the traffic buzz
through The Greenway,
high and low

glissandos of her footfalls play and dark
serenades her
starry skirt.

At dawn she crouches on the hand-carved seat
to waylay me,
make me swerve.

And can my running through Packsaddle Park
catch Ju de Lune
or does she sleep?

Night Visiting

i

Are sleepers in the dark visitable?
I mustn't disrupt her dream.
I'll stand at the door and look.

The meaning of aeon is sleep.
But sky is not a bed
and ours is lined with limestone.

ii

He stands at the door. Looks for her
during her aeon of sleep.

Makes certain. A husband must
but is she visitable?

She droops her head. She droops
like a pink water avens.

iii

Let me stand at their door and knock:
a widower's wife.

Hard-built grit in there.

I'm afraid to enter the house.
I'm afraid to make them wake.

She Walked Away

She had to

look forward to curtain a past
horizon where
home was

slipping down dull ragged
beaten ground dragging its light
bright enough that while it drowned
she could steer. Ray by ray

sun sank cold in the open
below North Downs but she couldn't
sleep just yet. She walked away

and doesn't sleep. She's awake
always,
and her day doesn't break.

Widow-walk

Widowman at our window
opens the lock.

I say it should be day.

> *I'm angry with the night*
> *withholding dawn.*

Widowman looks out
then flies to find her.

I ask where's day.

> *Is it behind the hill, the wall*
> *or is it in the wood?*

His widow-woman plunges
through wave-walls in rough seas.

He widow-walks for her until it's day.

Illyria by Rail

Evening: fur-
ragged sky bagging trees,
leaves dragging over pools stroked out of hiding

under ground.
Cosy up to strangers
while they listen to grandchildren, reading

Tripli-Cat
and Cat-Alogue, asking:
'The tooth fairy's note... was it in Mum's writing?'

They reply.
Point: 'Sea birds have arrived.
If there's a party in a field they're coming.

See that hedge?
The wrens hide there.' They say:
'What you know is what you choose to believe.' Turn

tightworded
away. Must we all leave
down the line lyrical lying where we will?

Learning to Be Together is an Old Pleasure

I'll wander with them both through Ways they wandered –
Covert Poplar Pinnacle and Tanglewood.

Relax. There's something wild about us now.
Tense suburban deer: those shingles smashed by trees

in yards overrun by their extensions.
We'll prance like the Boyntons who felled their house walls

and ate nuts. So Berkeley! All visitors
climb up old Remillard Rock praising its age,

eight hundred million years of it and we
can bum down Nut Hill's gold grass. Reel like Bambies

bumping and kicking at the rustbuckets,
beseeching: *Start Up Coachella. Go Love Bug.*

Moving On –

I was half-listening to the night
sounds of cars – on crises –
on essential works –

Reader – they slid me out of fear
to our car (unmendable –
so says the garage

church of free movement – but it goes)
Reader, you can't see our car –
you've seen your hand on

your own driver's door – your aches sink
to your stains as you read –
an owl taunted us –

who who who who who is driving
away at three a.m. –
driving toward what

the work is –

EPILOGUERY

Overheard

There's some disintegration you haven't done
that drapes the look of naked over bone.

There's some disintegration you haven't done.
You're flesh. Since mine has gone
I am only bone.
Can we discuss the absence of eye and brain
in seeing and knowing you? No skeleton
should be alone.
May we sit here a moment?
An old bowl in the sun.
Nakedness fits us all so don't
insist on more than a memory of skin.
I have lost my bare surface. I've had to learn
to drape the look of naked over bone.

Case Endings

Words change their forms like bodies:
widowman werwife

Does the third person singular
indicate equally 'he' 'she' or 'one'?
widow widow

Or a formal 'you'?
werhusband takewife

Could he/I/she be subjunctive?
wouldwife couldwife

Do 'we' have the present and/or the past?
triplecouple oncecouple doublecouple

Is every ending right?
wo/man wer/once

Can 'I' be objective
about 'them'…?
foundwife lostwife

Is this ending right
for 'us'…?
wefinders wekeepers

Whoever is being declined
is a person
she he me we us they him them

tense with language
dead or alive.
werwife oncewife Iwife

declinedandeverwillbewife

EPITAPHERY

Heaven is Nothing if Not Resolution

Now we are over, death
has nuanced our model of dead worlds.
Indeed, as some poet mentioned,
pearl is mere pavement here
    and no one dead mourns.

His first wife shakes her head:
    'You worriers. You pair!'
    How death grated.
    How slow we were
    to greet it as family.

She swirls through souls to find us:
    New Wife Judicious.
Our titles shatter and no longer matter.
    Husband Clarified.
Doesn't a song have trouble ending lines?

If tachyons of energy connected us
    held us like hands
    whirling in trinity
    laughing at finity –
'Us warriors of loss. Us!' –

then his lost wife never was distressed
nor was she ever calling her widower.
    So a buried heaven
    has grown us in its glove –
now, here in this herbery, let's love.

Milton Keynes UK
Ingram Content Group UK Ltd.
UKHW041157300823
427717UK00001B/54